The Insider's Guide:
7 Step to Get Into Nursing School

Laurie Robbins, BSN, RN, CBCN

Kindle Direct Publishing

Published by Kindle Direct Publishing.

All rights reserved.

No part of this book may be reproduced, or stored in a retrieval system, or transmitted in any form or by any means, electronic, mechanical, photocopying, recording, or otherwise, without express written permission of the author. For more information, please email laurierobbins@nursepreneurship.com.

ISBN-13: 978-1-7371371-0-8

Cover design by Laurie Robbins.

Dedication

To my husband and greatest love, my day one and #1 fan. To my children, the lights of my life. To my best friend of 30 years and into infinity. To my mother, my light and the sweetest woman I know. To my brother and my sister for their love and support. To all my family and friends. I love each of you for different and beautiful reasons, and that love is true and eternal.

Acknowledgements

From my very first day of nursing school to my most recent role transition into clinical education, there have been many incredible nursing instructors, nurse preceptors, mentors, educators, and colleagues who've shared their wealth of knowledge, imparted their wisdom, taught me their "tricks" and shortcuts, and, most importantly, exemplified remarkable humility and resilience. I am so grateful for every single person who I've had the extraordinary pleasure of working with through the years. You have each made me a better nurse, better educator, better mentor, better coach, and a better human.

Introduction

Growing up along the beautiful Gulf Coast of Texas in a small town of less than 1,000 people, I learned to entertain myself. My hobbies consisted of playing in the yard with my bunny rabbits, helping my mom plant and harvest her beloved garden vegetables, and slogging into the chicken coop to collect her coveted fresh eggs. Of course, I managed to accomplish all this while simultaneously annoying the crap out of her by jumping into every mud hole, splashing in every puddle, and bringing home every earthworm, caterpillar, lizard, frog, and garden snake I could get my hands on. Needless to say, there was never a dull moment in my house.

By the time I was 8 years old, I became interested in helping all kinds of wounded creatures, trying to "fix" them. I fashioned bandages out of leaves, securing them in place with long blades of grass, applying mud to their boo-boo's. And with that, I became a self-proclaimed animal doctor and my cherished backyard animal hospital was born. One day, after getting off the school bus, I went outside to play. Right there by the driveway, in the ditch (if you're from a small town, you know what this is), was a bird. It was a large bird with a big black beak, white neck, puffy white and gray body, gray wings with black tips, and some very crusty yellow-orange feet. I didn't know much about birds, but I knew if I walked up to it, it would probably fly away. So, of course I sashayed right over to the bird, but it didn't fly away. It screeched and squawked and flailed it's long birdy wings at me. That's when I realized that it must be hurt. Like any good animal doctor, I knew I had to help the poor little thing. So I reached down to pick it up and IT SNAPPED ITS CROOKED BEAK AT ME, pinching my pale skin between its beak parts.

After shrieking in fear and pain, I retrieved my throbbing hand, backed away, and ran into the house crying hysterically. As my mom examined my hand, I explained that a horrible demon-possessed bird had just terrorized me. While she rubbed a freshly-harvested aloe leaf on it and wiped my tears, I collected my thoughts and decided that fixing animals was not the right path for me. I made a bold decision then and there that I would use my gift of healing and desire to help others to take care of *people* instead. This decision finalized when, in 5th grade, after lovingly raising dozens of chickens for my 4-H project, they were sold to the highest bidder for their meat, and I was asked to slaughter and clean them all within the week. Needless to say, I've never looked at chicken the same way since.

  Once I entered high school, my focus narrowed and I decided that a career in nursing was in my future. I joined HOSA (Health Occupation Students of America), became a certified nursing assistant in a local hospital, and fell in love with caring for people, interacting with patients and families, and seeing the camaraderie and teamwork of the nursing and medical staff.

After sharing my dream with my family, I found out that nursing was in my blood - my grandmother had also been a nurse during World War II and the Vietnam War. I knew that if she did it, so could I. If I was going to do it, I would have to go all in. So I did.

And now we come to my reason for writing this book. For me, preparing for, applying to, and surviving nursing school was challenging, to say the least. My goal for this book is to shed light on the process, give you some tips and ideas that worked for me along the way, and hopefully turn on some light bulbs in that beautiful brain of yours to help you think about the process in a different way. By the time you're done reading this book, you will have everything you need to prepare for and get into nursing school, and be a confident and successful nursing student.

I'm going to share my experiences, advice, research, and a bunch of common sense stuff I've picked up along the way. I will share with you how to prepare for a future in nursing, how to choose and apply for nursing school, and share some tips and insight to help you not only survive but thrive through your nursing program.

I hope you are as excited to keep reading as I am to be writing this book. I know we are going to have a great time so let's get started!

Table of Contents

Introduction

Step 1: Know Your "Why"

Step 2: Purpose & Prerequisites

Step 3: Prepare Yourself

Step 4: Choose a School

Step 5: Application Process

Step 6: Plan for Success

Step 7: Time to Thrive!

Conclusion

Step 1: Know Your "Why"

Now that I've opened up about my path to nursing, let's talk about yours and why you purchased this book. Whether you've wanted to be a nurse your entire life, you're fed up with your job, you want to take care of people, or you want a career that is more stable with excellent pay, benefits, and travel opportunities, nursing is an excellent choice. There are very few careers more fulfilling, rewarding, or amazing than nursing. So whatever your reason, I want you to hold onto it as we begin to unpack all the things you need to know about becoming a nurse.

But before we get into the meat of it, let's talk about some important things you need to consider before beginning the process. First, nursing is not for everyone. If you don't like people, you should definitely not become a nurse. If you don't like following policies, laws, regulations, and instructions, nursing is also not for you. If you faint and convulse at the sight of a needle or speck of blood, nursing might not be the best choice for you. And finally, if you crave the spotlight and want glory and fame, nursing is definitely not the right line of work for you.

Now let's talk about what nursing is. Nursing is about caring, doing the right thing even when it's the hardest thing, and always advocating for your patient no matter the circumstances. Nursing is about being part of a team of diverse people from different disciplines and backgrounds, all trying to improve or save a life, though they don't always succeed. Nursing is about delivering the very best care to every single human being in the exact same way NO MATTER WHAT. Nursing is about putting aside your own personal beliefs and values to provide care while respecting your patient's beliefs and values.

Nursing is about uplifting the nurses around you when they are struggling, when their patient dies, or when, as with recent events, a global pandemic arises and all you can do is show up every day and put one foot in front of the other. Nursing is about teaching - the patients, their families, the community, other nurses, doctors, and staff. Nursing is about learning - about your patients, the diseases that plague them, the cultures that seek care in your community, and the disparities that plague our healthcare system.

Nursing is about doing the right thing when no one is watching because it's the right thing to do. Nursing is about people - ALL people, your people, my people, his people, her people, all the people. If you do not want to care, show empathy, be brave, fight for what is right, give your all when sometimes it's still not enough, then please pick another career. Because

I can tell you, without a doubt, that nursing is 100% most certainly NOT FOR YOU.

Now that we've gotten that out of the way and you're still reading, that's a good sign that you've made a great decision. What I am going to share with you in the rest of this book will hopefully help you make informed and smart decisions so you can move forward with confidence and be successful.

Step 2: Purpose & Prerequisites

Now that we've established that you do, in fact, still want to be a nurse, let's talk about how to get into nursing school. The very best thing you could've done is buy this book and get answers to your most burning questions. If you are still in high school, go talk to your guidance counselor. If you're getting ready to start college or are already attending, go talk to an academic advisor. Both are there to help you map out a plan and get you on the path toward your goals. Below are my best tips.

Any science course is a sure bet - biology, anatomy, chemistry, physiology, microbiology - pretty much any science class that ends in "y" should be on your schedule. Statistics is a MUST and a prerequisite for every nursing program I've seen. Any class related to health, wellness, human growth and development, or something in those categories are encouraged as well. Also, if your high school offers a health occupations program like HOSA, you should definitely consider taking that course and working the part-time job, if feasible. You will learn so much and this will give you some experience working in a healthcare setting, and will also look great on your resume as you apply for your first healthcare or nursing job.

If you are in college, or soon will be, make sure you take the following classes before you start your nursing program: nutrition, pharmacology, dosage calculations, psychology, and critical thinking. Most, if not all, of these classes will count toward either the required prerequisites for the program you choose or can be used as required elective courses toward your nursing degree, especially in bachelor programs.

Required prerequisites for practically every nursing program across the country include anatomy and physiology 1 & 2 with lab (2 semesters), general chemistry with lab, microbiology with lab, and statistics, if not taken already as mentioned above. These are pretty much standard across the board for both associate and bachelor degree nursing programs. Most programs require that these credits are within five years or less of the date you apply, so take them right before you apply. Keep in mind, every nursing program has different requirements so do your research.

Step 3: Prepare Yourself

Now that we've talked about which classes you should take, let's discuss some housekeeping items. Once you are accepted into a nursing program, you will be asked to complete a background check and get your fingerprints recorded. This is done for three reasons: 1) to ensure that you qualify to sit for the licensing exam and be licensed by your state; 2) healthcare organizations require a clean background before allowing you to complete your clinical training in their facility; and 3) to hire you as a new graduate nurse. Now it's time to tie up any loose ends such as outstanding traffic violations, warrants, bad checks, etc. (if this applies to you). These things will catch up to you, so take care of them now.

Now it's time to start planning for your transition into nursing school. Whether you're graduating from high school, a college student with a summer job, or a full-time 40-hour employee, you need a transition plan. Going to nursing school and working full time is nearly impossible and highly discouraged. Class schedules and clinical training may be days, evenings, or even weekends with little to no flexibility offered. If you can get by without working, or only working a few part-time hours, these are the best scenarios. If you have health insurance, get your annual check-up now; you'll need a physical to submit with your application and you'll need certain vaccines before beginning clinical training, so get those, too. Go to the dentist and get your annual cleaning and exam done. Just take care of all these things now so they won't cause problems for you later.

Most nursing programs require a minimum GPA, minimum science grades in your college coursework, and a minimum score on the HESI® A2, TEAS®, or other entrance exam to even be considered for their program. These exams test your vocabulary, general knowledge, reading comprehension, grammar, math, chemistry, biology, physics, and anatomy and physiology. There is also a section for identifying your learning style and personality. You will likely also take this exam, or a version of it, more than once during your program. Find a study guide that fits your needs and start studying.

The last, but most important, tip I will leave you is to get in the right mindset to be successful. If you are a "negative Nelly", are a constant worrier, have test anxiety, like being in control, or find social settings difficult, you should begin working on your mindset now. There are plenty of books, podcasts, courses, etc., on this and other personal development topics. Ask for recommendations, visit the library, Google search, or whatever you need to do to find content. Then implement and continually practice what you find most helpful. Positive affirmations, mindfulness, daily gratitude, and even meditation are just a few of the practices you can integrate into your life to make every day, every task, and every challenge easier to face and overcome.

Step 4: Choose a School

If you already know which school you want to attend, you're halfway there! If not, it's time to start making your list. Do you prefer traditional in person classes or do you want to attend class virtually? With all of the recent advances in technology and learning platforms, you can complete your program almost totally online, except for the clinical training component. And there are many options, including community college, online-only programs, and traditional universities, each offering multiple class formats to choose from.

Once you've got an idea of the course format, visit your state's board of nursing (BON) website. There you will find a list of all the accredited nursing programs operating in your state, grouped by degree type - diploma, associates, bachelors, etc. Also included are the nursing program's current status, what tracks the program offers, program contact information, as well as recent NCLEX (RN licensing exam) pass rates. At the end of the day, it is your responsibility to make sure the program is accredited.

The best next step is to make a list of your top 5-10 schools and their admission requirements and nursing program prerequisites. Once you have all this information, you can see what you still need (if anything) to qualify for each program, or which programs you already qualify to apply for. If you have already completed some college coursework, request a transfer credit evaluation to see what credits transfer into the nursing program you chose. My suggestion is to pick the school that will take the most transfer credits, has an acceptable NCLEX pass rating, and can get you through the program in the least amount of time.

Step 5: Application Process

The application process is straightforward but will require attention to detail and organization. Have all the required application documents in order and make yourself AT LEAST 2 COMPLETE COPIES. If your paperwork is messy, wrinkled, coffee stained, or otherwise tarnished, it will reflect poorly on you during the selection process. This is not the time two do things halfway. This is the time to be detail oriented and ridiculously meticulous. Before you turn in your final packet for submission, make sure you keep the copies handy in case the school asks you for additional paperwork or tells you something is missing.

Do not leave anything to chance. Don't be late turning in your application - they will not make an exception for any reason whatsoever. If you have to take the day off, arrange it. You will likely have to turn in your own packet and sign their receipt. Don't give them the chance to be picky or exclude your application for any reason.

Also, don't put all your eggs in one basket. Apply to every program for which you qualify. That way, you are much more likely to get into at least one of them, and possibly more than one, and then you can choose the best one for you. If all the schools have great ratings, are accredited, and have similar NCLEX pass rates, you really can't go wrong.

Once the applications have been processed and final candidates narrowed, some nursing programs have an additional interview requirement. I don't see this being done for 2-year associate degree programs, but is often done for bachelor degree programs where there is more competition and a large number of applicants. Just be yourself, answer the questions honestly, and do your best.

Step 6: Plan for Success

You did it - you got accepted into the nursing school of your dreams! If you're anything like me, when you saw that letter your stomach turned several somersaults and you got a bit nauseous. Then you read it and either shrieked in delight or ugly cried joyful tears. I actually did both, which thoroughly freaked out my family, who all thought I was having a complete mental breakdown.

After the initial shock subsided, I really began to freak out thinking what in the world I was going to do about my job, my bills, my life, which was about to completely change virtually overnight. There will be some things you need to figure out as well, which is why I mentioned this in Chapter 2, so you would be ready.

I worked a few PRN jobs to make ends meet. When they hired me, I told my employers that my work schedule would be dependent on my nursing school schedule. If they are healthcare jobs (patient care technician, medical office assistant, etc.) they will understand. The best piece of advice I will give in this book is to get a job in a hospital, since they can provide the most flexibility. Also, it can be difficult to get your first nursing job with no experience. But if you're already working in a hospital, they are much more willing to hire you into their nurse residency program than someone from outside the organization.

    This brings me to another important point in this section - don't be afraid to ask for help. Your friends and family will do what they can to help, if they are able, and they love you. Just file away their generosity for later, and when you get on your feet, you can return the favor.

Step 7: Time to Thrive!

WOO HOO! The first day of the rest of your life is finally here! Day one of nursing school is a whirlwind and a blur. Let's first discuss the volumes of books and study guides you will be asked to purchase for your first semester. You can certainly head over to the bookstore and buy the still-wrapped-in-plastic, brand new books, full of new-book-smell. However, you do not need to buy brand new books. Consider purchasing used books or even renting them. The campus bookstore as well as any number of online bookstores carry both used and rentable books. As long as you have the correct version, volume or revision, that's all that matters. Save your money for more important things, like midnight snacks and anything caffeinated.

Plan your week, month, or even semester. You will probably go to lecture class 3 days a week and have clinical training 2 days a week. You will study most of your waking hours and sleep when you can. Self-care is going to be challenging but necessary. Work in some time for physical activity, which relieves stress. Consider meal planning and so you can grab and go. And always carry snacks because you just never know. Plan study sessions with peers, which are great opportunities to bounce around ideas and share stories that may help someone through a rough patch. Finally, pencil in a few hours each week for something NOT related to nursing. Go to the movies, grab coffee, go on a drive, ride go-carts - anything to free your mind and give yourself a moment to forget all about the chaos and just be yourself. Your mind, body and soul need it - you will thank me later. Just remember, you will prioritize what is most important, so don't forget to put yourself on that list.

    Nursing school will be one of the most challenging experiences of your life. But you will absolutely get through it, just like the many who came before you. Remember to breathe, take lots of study breaks, don't stress about things outside of your control, give yourself a break, and pass on what you learn to the next generation of nurses that will come after you.

Conclusion

Now you've got all you need to put a plan in place and start working toward your goals. Set yourself up for success by following the tips provided and you will do well. There are plenty of study guides, mnemonics, and other helpful publications out there to get you through nursing school material, the NCLEX exam, and even help you prepare your resume to land your first nursing job, so find the ones that match your learning style.

    I am developing additional organizational tools and study guides as well, so if you like my writing and want to see more, please visit my website at www.nursepreneurship.com or email me at laurierobbins@nursepreneurship.com for more information. Check back soon and often so you don't miss out on new content!

Thank you for your support. I wish you success into and throughout nursing school, and into your first nursing job and beyond. I look forward to seeing you in the nursing profession one day soon!

www.ingramcontent.com/pod-product-compliance
Lightning Source LLC
Chambersburg PA
CBHW070803050426
42452CB00012B/2477